Reconciliation
Pardon and Peace

"Repent, and believe in the gospel."

MARK 1:15b

General Editors

Sister Catherine Dooley, O.P.

Monsignor Thomas McDade, Ed.D.

RCL
Benziger®

The Subcommittee on the Catechism,
United States Conference of Catholic Bishops, has found this
catechetical series, copyright 2015, to be in conformity with the
Catechism of the Catholic Church.

Nihil Obstat: Sister Karen Wilhelmy, CSJ, Censor Deputatus

Imprimatur: † Roger Cardinal Mahony, Archbishop of Los Angeles, September 2005

The nihil obstat and imprimatur are official declarations that the work contains nothing contrary to Faith and Morals. It is not implied, thereby, that those who have granted the nihil obstat and imprimatur agree with the contents, statements, or opinions expressed.

Acknowledgments

Consultants: James Gaffney, Enrico Hernandez, Monica Hughes, David Michael Thomas
Contributors: Jane Ayer, Sylvia DeVillers, Janie Gustafson, Marianne Lenihan, Joanne McPortland, Margaret Savitskas, Rita Burns Senseman
Music: Gary Daigle
Spanish: José Segovia, María Elena Carrión
Scripture passages are taken from the *New American Bible with Revised New Testament. Revised New Testament of the New American Bible,* copyright © 1986 by the Confraternity of Christian Doctrine, Washington, D.C. All rights reserved. *Old Testament of the New American Bible,* copyright © 1970 by the Confraternity of Christian Doctrine, Washington, D.C. No part of the *Revised New Testament of the New American Bible* can be reproduced in any form without permission in writing from the copyright owner. *Lectionary for Masses with Children,* Cycles A, B, C, and Weekdays, copyright © 1994, Archdiocese of Chicago, Liturgy Training Publications. All rights reserved.

Excerpts from the English translation of the *Roman Missal* © 2010, International Commission on English in the Liturgy (ICEL). Excerpts from *Catholic Household Blessings and Prayers* (revised edition), © 2007, United States Conference of Catholic Bishops.

Send all inquiries to:
RCL Benziger
8805 Governor's Hill Drive • Suite 400
Cincinnati, OH 45249

Toll Free   877-275-4725
Fax   800-688-8356
Visit us at RCLBenziger.com
and RCLBSacraments.com

30846   ISBN 978-0-7829-1691-1

Table of Contents

Welcome!

This is a special time for you and your family. You are taking one more step on your journey with Jesus.

This book will help you as you prepare to celebrate the Sacrament of Penance and Reconciliation for the first time. You will learn how much God loves you. You will practice choices and actions that show your love for God and others. You will come to know that God is merciful and forgiving. Even when people turn away from God's love, he is always ready to welcome them back. The Sacrament of Penance and Reconciliation celebrates God's love, forgiveness, and mercy.

Many people in your parish will be praying for you as you prepare to celebrate the Sacrament of Penance and Reconciliation for the first time. You are surrounded by a whole community who can show you how to live in God's love. May God bless you and keep you close.

God's Love

What will separate us from the love of Christ?

ROMANS 8:35

Everyone is Here

It was time to return to the school. The field trip to the science center was over.

Mrs. Wilson counted each child on the bus. ". . . 22, 23, 24. Everyone is here!

Let's go!" she said to the bus driver.

"Why do you count everyone?" asked Patrick.

"I don't want to leave anyone behind," answered Mrs. Wilson with a smile. "I care about you too much!"

■ How do you think her words made Patrick feel?

■ What are some things people do because they love you?

The Lost Sheep

Everyone wants to be loved and cared for. Jesus wanted people to understand how much God loves them. Jesus thought of a way to help people know about God's love. He told a simple story about a shepherd and a lost sheep. Read the story Jesus told.

"If any of you has a hundred sheep, and one of them gets lost, what will you do?

"Won't you leave the ninety-nine in the field and go look for the lost sheep until you find it?

"And when you find it, you will be so glad that you will put it on your shoulder and carry it home.

"Then you will call in your friends and neighbors and say, 'Let's celebrate! I've found my lost sheep.' "

BASED ON LUKE 15:4–6

The people listened to Jesus' story with great interest. They understood the words of Jesus. God is like the shepherd who cares for every sheep in the flock. God watches over all people. God loves them and cares for them, even when they wander away like a lost sheep! Even when they turn away from his love, God continues to love his people.

Let's Talk

- Why do you think the shepherd went after the one sheep who wandered away?

- How is God like the shepherd in Jesus' story?

- How does this story help you to think about God's love?

God Saves

The Bible also tells the story of Adam and Eve, the first people. They chose to turn away from God's love. They wandered away like the sheep in Jesus' story.

The choice of Adam and Eve to say "no" to God is called **Original Sin**. Because of this choice, sadness, suffering, and death came into God's good creation. That first sin not only lost original holiness for Adam and Eve, but for all humankind as well.

God did not give up on his people. God our Father sent his Son, Jesus, into the world to save all people. Jesus gave his life to bring all people back to God's love. Jesus' sacrifice made it possible for us to have eternal life with God. The name Jesus means "God saves."

Baptism

In the Sacrament of **Baptism,** the Church celebrates this saving love of God. Baptism takes away Original Sin. Baptism gives people new life with God. This new life is called grace. **Grace** is God's own life and love alive in you.

In Baptism you became a follower of Jesus and a member of the Church. You were marked as God's own child forever. In the Sacrament of Penance and Reconciliation you renew your Baptism. Any sins committed after Baptism are forgiven.

9

We Are Disciples

Your Story

Prepare your own story about God's love for you. In Baptism, you became a follower of Jesus and a member of the Church. What are some things you will do to show your love and care for God and for others?

Draw or write your story in the outline of the sheep.

Parish Connection

Look for the baptismal font or pool in your church. Make the Sign of the Cross with holy water to remind you of your Baptism.

We Are God's People

Leader Let us remember God's love for us.

All In the name of the Father, and of the Son, and of the Holy Spirit. Amen.

Leader Let us pray.

All We are God's people,
the sheep of his flock.

Leader You know the Lord is God!
He created us,
and we belong to him;
we are his people,
the sheep in his pasture.

All We are God's people,
the sheep of his flock.

Leader The Lord is good!
His love and faithfulness
will last forever.

All We are God's people,
the sheep of his flock.

BASED ON PSALM 100:3, 5

Home and Family

Family Note

Dear Family,

I have learned about God's love for us. The Bible tells how Adam and Eve turned away from God's love. God our Father sent his Son, Jesus, to save us. In Baptism we celebrate God's saving love. Baptism takes away Original Sin and gives us a new life of grace as members of the Church. The Sacrament of Penance and Reconciliation renews our Baptism.

Family Chat

Talk as a family about the ways God shows love for all of you.

On Your Own

Make up your own prayer or song of thanks for God's love.

With Your Family

Ask your parents to share memories of your Baptism. Have an adult light your baptismal candle or another candle as a reminder. Teach family members the prayer or song of thanks that you made up.

RCLBsacraments.com

2

Loving God

Teach me to do your will, for you are my God.

Mom's Rule

Eric jumped into the back seat of his mom's car. He couldn't wait to get to his first soccer practice. Eric was so excited!

"You know the rule: Buckle your seat belt," Eric's mom said, before she started the car.

"Yeah," Eric's older sister, Jessie, said in a bossy voice. "It's the law. Mom will get a ticket if you don't!"

"That's not the only reason," said Eric's mother. She turned and gave Eric a smile. "I want you to be safe. That's why we have the rule."

Eric smiled back, buckling his seat belt with a loud click.

- Why did Eric's mom have a rule about seat belts?

- What are some rules that your family has?

- How do rules show our love for one another?

What Must I Do?

Following rules is not always easy to do. Sometimes it seems like there are too many rules. People who lived in the time of Jesus must have felt that way. One day, as Jesus was traveling to Jerusalem and teaching along the way, he met a man who asked him an interesting question. Read the story from the Bible to find out the question.

An expert in the Law of Moses stood up and asked Jesus a question.

"Teacher," he said. "What must I do to have eternal life?"

Jesus answered, "What is written in the Scriptures? How do you understand them?"

The man replied, "The Scriptures say 'Love the Lord your God with all your heart, soul, strength, and mind.' They also say, 'Love your neighbors as much as you love yourself.'"

Jesus said, "You have given the right answer. If you do this, you will have eternal life."

BASED ON LUKE 10:25–28

Let's Talk

■ What does the Scripture say about loving God?

■ What does it say about loving your neighbor? Who is your neighbor?

■ Give an example of how you can show love to your neighbor.

Loving God

God wants all people to be happy forever. Long ago, God made a holy promise, or **covenant**, with his people. He promised to be with his people always. God said, "I will be your God, and you will be my people" (Leviticus 26:12).

God gave his people rules or laws to follow. These laws are the **Ten Commandments**. Jesus taught people how to live up to the promises made to God. Jesus reminded people about obeying the Ten Commandments. When you obey God's Laws, you are showing your love for God and for one another.

Turn to page 85 in *A Little Catechism* for a review of the Ten Commandments.

The Great Commandment

You show your love for God when you love other people. Jesus told people that the way to **eternal life**, or happiness forever with God, is the way of love. As a follower of Jesus, you are to love other people as you love yourself.

This teaching of Jesus about love is called the **Great Commandment:**

Love God above all things, and love your neighbor as you love yourself.

You do what the Great Commandment tells you to do when you live the Ten Commandments. The first three Commandments help you to love and respect God. The other seven Commandments help you to love and respect others.

Activity

You are a follower of Jesus Christ. You listen to his words. What is one thing you can do to show your love for God? What is one way you can show love for other people?

Draw or write your answers in the hearts.

GOD

OTHERS

We Are Disciples

Activity Walking the Way of Love

Remember the words of the Great Commandment.

Using a pencil or pen, begin at "Start" and follow the path that takes you down the way of love.

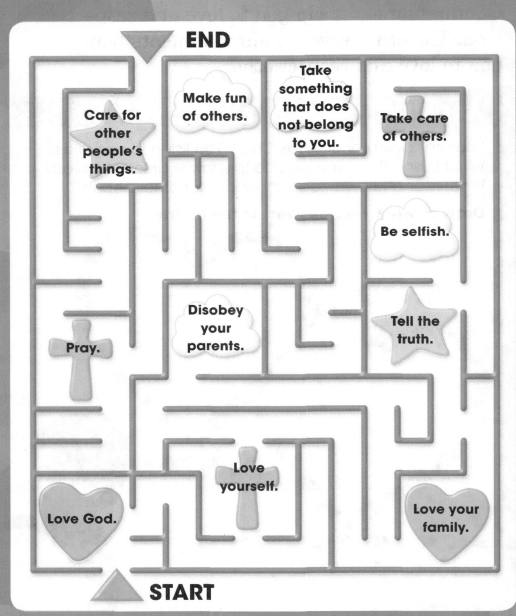

END

Care for other people's things.

Make fun of others.

Take something that does not belong to you.

Take care of others.

Be selfish.

Disobey your parents.

Tell the truth.

Pray.

Love yourself.

Love God.

Love your family.

START

Parish Connection

When you go to Mass on Sunday, you are obeying the Third Commandment.

What happens when you do not follow the way of love?

Give Us Light

All
Lord, give us light
to walk the way of love.

Leader
The Law of the Lord is perfect;
it gives us new life.
His teachings last forever,
and they give wisdom to his people.

All
Lord, give us light
to walk the way of love.

Leader
The Lord's instruction is right;
it makes our hearts glad.
His commands shine brightly,
they give us light.

All
Lord, give us light
to walk the way of love.

Leader
Let our words and our thoughts
be pleasing to you, Lord,
because you are our mighty rock
and our protector.

All
Lord, give us light
to walk the way of love.

BASED ON PSALM 19:8, 9, 15

Home and Family

Family Note

Dear Family,

I learned that long ago God made a covenant, or holy promise. God gave his people the Ten Commandments. I learned that God wants me to love him and to love other people. This is the Great Commandment. I can show my love by obeying the Ten Commandments and following the teachings of Jesus. If I show my love in this way, God promises I will be happy with him forever.

Family Chat

Talk about ways family members follow the Great Commandment every day.

On Your Own

Make a calendar for the week. At the end of each day, draw one heart on the calendar for each loving action you did for God or for others. Try to fill your calendar with hearts!

RCLBsacraments.com

With Your Family

Make up a list of family commandments that will help you show love for God and for one another. Decorate the list, and display it where family members can see it.

3

Oh, that today you would hear his voice:
Do not harden your hearts . . . PSALM 95:7–8

I Say "No!"

Has this ever happened to you?
I know what I'm supposed to do,
To be a friend, to let love show,
But I do the reverse—I just say "No!"

I know the rules I should obey,
But sometimes I want my own way.
Instead of doing what is right,
I say "No!" I choose to fight!

The people that I love the most
I sometimes hurt. I'm mean, I boast,
I'm selfish, angry—yet I know
I hurt myself, too,
when I say "No!"

- Have you ever felt like the speaker in the poem?

- What are the ways you hurt others when you say "No"?

- How do you hurt yourself?

Failing to Love

Jesus showed us how we should love God and others. Jesus also taught about the end of time. Jesus said that at the Last Judgment he will judge all people on the way they lived their lives. He will look at how people have loved others. Those who turn their backs on others may be surprised. They will learn that they have turned their backs on God. Here is what Jesus said:

"Then the king will say to those on his left,

'Get away from me! I was hungry, but you did not give me anything to eat, and I was thirsty, but you did not give me anything to drink. I was a stranger, but you did not welcome me, and I was naked, but you did not give me any clothes to wear. I was sick and in jail, but you did not take care of me.'

"Then the people will ask,

'Lord, when did we fail to help you when you were hungry or thirsty or a stranger or naked or sick or in jail?'

"The king will say to them,

'Whenever you failed to help any of my people, no matter how unimportant they seemed, you failed to do it for me.'"

BASED ON MATTHEW 25:41–45

Loving Choices

Talk about ways that people do not treat others with love. Talk about ways people can show love to others. With a partner, act out one way people say "No" to God's love. Then act out a more loving choice.

Sin and Forgiveness

God created you and he loves you. But God does not force you to love him. He does not force you to love others. God gave you **free will**. You can choose to say "Yes" or "No" to love and to God's Laws.

Sin is turning your back on God's love and doing what you know is wrong. You can also sin by not doing what you know is right or loving. The people in Jesus' story sinned by not showing love for others. Like the people in the Bible story, you will be judged individually on how well you have loved.

God wants you to act in a loving way. When you choose sin instead of love, you are choosing your own way instead of God's way. You are breaking the promises made at your Baptism. You are turning away from God's grace.

Sin Hurts

Sin hurts your relationship with God and with others. **Mortal sin** is very serious. Mortal sin cuts you off from God. Less serious sins are called **venial sins**. Venial sins weaken your relationships with God and with other people.

Celebrating Forgiveness

God's **mercy** is stronger than any sin. When you are sorry for your sins and promise to do better, God is always ready to forgive you. God wants to fill your life with love and grace again. The Church celebrates God's forgiveness in the Sacrament of **Penance and Reconciliation**. This Sacrament is also called **Penance** or **Reconciliation**. The word *reconciliation* means "coming back together in peace." The word *penance* means "making up for doing wrong." When you celebrate the Sacrament of Penance and Reconciliation, you receive the grace to live as God wants you to live. You celebrate this Sacrament for the first time before you receive First Eucharist.

We Are Disciples

Activity Wrong Choices

You cannot sin by accident or by mistake. If you do something because you are afraid or someone forces you to do something, it may not be a sin. Sin is a wrong choice that you make.

Circle the sentences in which a sin takes place.

Right

Wrong

Parish Connection

At Mass, listen for the prayers that praise God's mercy. Say **"Lord, have mercy"** and **"Christ, have mercy"** after the priest does.

Your mom won't give you money for some candy so you take money from her purse when she is out of the room.

You trip on the playground and knock over a small child.

You make fun of a classmate who has trouble making friends.

You are helping to clean up after dinner. One of the dishes slips out of your hands and breaks.

What Does God Do?

Listen to the leader of prayer read these words. Close your eyes and think about what sin is as you listen.

[Each] one of us has been baptized, and so we are all sons and daughters of God. God loves us as a Father, and he asks us to love him with all our hearts. He also wants us to be good to each other, so that we may all live happily together.

But people do not always do what God wants. They say, "I will not obey! I am going to do as I please." They disobey God and do not want to listen to him. We, too, often act like that.

. . . What does God do when someone turns away from him? What does he do when we leave the path of goodness that he has shown us, when we run the risk of losing the life of grace he has given us? Does God turn away from us when we turn away from him by our sins?

Here is what God does, in the words of Jesus himself:

Heaven is filled with joy when one sinner turns back to God.

(LUKE 15:7)

RITE OF PENANCE, APPENDIX II 46 AND 47

In the quiet of your heart, tell God you are sorry for the times you have not chosen to love.

Home and Family

Family Note

Dear Family,

I have learned that sin is a choice to turn away from God's love. All sin hurts. Serious sin cuts people off from God. Less serious sin weakens my friendship with God and others. God always wants to forgive sin when I am sorry and promise to do better. The Sacrament of Penance and Reconciliation celebrates God's mercy and forgiveness.

Family Chat

Ask family members for ideas on how to say "No" to sin and "Yes" to love.

On Your Own

Who are the people in your life who are looking for love from you? Choose one way to show your love to someone this week.

With Your Family

Talk about what you can do to help people who need food or warm clothes. Show your love by helping others as a family.

RCLBsacraments.com

4

Loving Choices

My portion is the LORD;
  I promise to keep your words.   PSALM 119:57

You Decide

Every day Lisa walks home from school with her friend Maria and Maria's big sister. One day Maria asks Lisa to come to her house to watch a movie.

Lisa is supposed to go straight home after school and start her homework. Her grandmother will be waiting for her. But Lisa really wants to watch the movie, so she goes to Maria's house.

"Do you want to call your grandmother?" Maria's sister asks Lisa. Lisa knows that if she does not call, her grandmother will worry. But if she does call, Grandma will tell Lisa to come home right away.

Decide how this story will end. In a small group, talk about what you think Lisa will do. What will happen if Lisa makes this choice?

On Solid Rock

Jesus wanted people to know how important it was to make good choices. He told this story:

"Anyone who hears and obeys these teachings of mine is like a wise person who built a house on solid rock.

Rain poured down, rivers flooded, and winds beat against that house. But it did not fall, because it was built on solid rock.

Anyone who hears my teachings and does not obey them is like a foolish person who built a house on sand.

The rain poured down, the rivers flooded, and the winds blew and beat against that house. Finally, it fell with a crash."

BASED ON MATTHEW 7:24–27

What message is Jesus giving about wise and unwise choices?

What is the message?

In groups of three, act out a scene of people making good choices or bad choices. Below are some suggestions for situations you might act out.

1. **You and your brother are throwing a ball in the house. You are not supposed to play ball in the house. A vase gets knocked over and breaks.**

   Choice 1: Tell your mom you are sorry for playing ball in the house and breaking the vase.

   Choice 2: Bury the broken pieces in the trash and tell your mom you don't know what happened when she asks about it.

2. **A new student comes to your class.**

   Choice 1: You and your friend laugh at her because you don't like her clothes.

   Choice 2: You and your friend ask her to play with you at recess.

Making Choices

You make choices all the time. Some choices are easy, like deciding whether to have an apple or a banana for a snack. Other choices are more difficult. You may need to make what is called a moral choice. This is a choice between something that is right and something that is wrong. Knowing the difference is not always as easy as choosing between apples and bananas!

How can you make good moral choices? Try following these steps:

- Stop and think about the choice you are making. Which choice would show love for God and others?

- Think about what will happen if you make each choice. Your choices have consequences. This means that your choices can help or hurt you and others.

- Think of God's Laws. Ask the Holy Spirit to help you make the best choice.

Your Solid Rock

You do not have to make choices without help. God has given you the gift of a **conscience** to help you make moral choices. Your conscience is your inner sense of what is right and what is wrong. Your conscience helps you remember what you have learned from your family, your teachers, and the Church about what is right.

The Ten Commandments and the teachings of Jesus help guide your conscience.

In a way, your conscience can be like the solid rock in Jesus' story. Use it wisely and you will make good moral choices. Ignore what you know is right, and you will make choices that are foolish or even sinful. It's up to you.

Let's Talk

■ Give examples of a moral choice you might make.

■ Why should you think about the consequences?

■ How does your conscience help you choose?

■ Who can you ask for advice?

We Are Disciples

Activity On Rock or Sand?

Read each choice.
Circle the rock if you think it is a moral, or right choice.
Circle the sand if you think it is a wrong choice.

Will steals a candy bar from the store.

Ben gives up a trip to the park with his friends to spend time with his grandmother, who is visiting.

Janie forgets to study her spelling words, so she copies Teresa's paper.

Bill admits he broke his brother's toy by accident. He offers his brother one of his own favorite toys to make up for it.

Justin took five dollars out of his older brother's drawer.

Sue said some mean things to Mary that made Mary feel very sad.

Cindy broke a flowerpot, but she said Julie did it.

Your friend broke your favorite toy by accident. You get angry and break one of his.

34

We Come Before Our Father

Leader God, our Father, sometimes we have not behaved as your children should.

All But you love us and come to us.

Leader We have given trouble to our parents and teachers.

All But you love us and come to us.

Leader We have quarrelled and called each other names.

All But you love us and come to us.

Leader We have been lazy at home and in school, and have not been helpful to our [families].

All But you love us and come to us.

Leader We have thought too much of ourselves and have told lies.

All But you love us and come to us.

Leader We have not done good to others when we had the chance.

All But you love us and come to us.

Leader Now with Jesus, our brother, we come before our Father in Heaven and ask him to forgive our sins:

All Our Father . . .

RITE OF PENANCE APPENDIX II 50

Home and Family

Family Note

Dear Family,

I have learned that a moral choice is a choice between right and wrong. I know that it is important to think about the consequences of my choices, and to ask for God's help in making good choices. I have a conscience that helps me choose what is right. What I have learned from you and from the Church helps to form and to guide my conscience.

Family Chat

Talk about how to make good choices.

On Your Own

Make up your own examination of conscience. Think about the choices you made and the things you did this week. How do they measure up against what your conscience tells you is right?

With Your Family

Talk about the choices characters make on TV shows or in the movies. Are these moral choices? What steps do the characters follow when they make their choices? What are the consequences? What would you do differently?

 RCLBsacraments.com

Returning to Love

> LORD, have mercy on me; heal me,
> I have sinned against you.   PSALM 41:5

The Right Words

I got so mad when I lost the game,
I called my friend an awful name.
My friend acted really hurt,
But I just laughed, and made it worse.
Now he's gone, and I'm so lonely.
He'd come back, I know, if only
I could find the words to say
To make my bad words go away!

Pretend you are the speaker of this poem.

- What can you say or do to make up with your friend?

- Share your ideas with a partner.

Going Home

Jesus wanted people to know that God's love is always waiting, even when people turn away. So Jesus told a story about a young man who ran away from home. The young man wasted his family's money on selfish choices. Then, when he was poor and alone, the runaway's heart changed. Jesus continued the story:

"Finally, he came to his senses and said, 'My father's workers have plenty to eat, and here I am, starving to death! I will leave and go to my father and say to him, "Father, I have sinned against God in heaven and against you. I am no longer good enough to be called your son. Treat me like one of your workers.""

"The younger son got up and started back to his father. But when he was still a long way off, his father saw him and felt sorry for him. He ran to his son and hugged and kissed him.

"The son said, 'Father, I have sinned against God in heaven and against you. I am no longer good enough to be called your son.'

"But his Father said to the servants, 'Hurry and bring the best clothes and put them on him. Give him a ring for his finger and sandals for his feet. Get the best calf and prepare it, so we can eat and celebrate. This son of mine was dead, but has now come back to life. He was lost and has now been found.' And they began to celebrate."

BASED ON LUKE 15:17–24

Let's Talk

How is God like the father of the runaway in Jesus' story?

Being Sorry

In the story that Jesus told, the son returned home and said he was sorry. How do you make up with a friend you've hurt? You can admit you were wrong. You can say, "I'm sorry." You can ask your friend to forgive you. You can promise to be a better friend. And you can do whatever you can to make up for what you did.

When you sin, you hurt yourself and others. You hurt your friendship with God. But sin is not the end. To restore and strengthen your friendship with God, follow the same steps you would follow with your friend.

- **Admit you were wrong.** Admit that you made wrong choices.

- **Say you are sorry.** The sorrow you feel for sin is called **contrition**.

- **Ask God's forgiveness.** The best part is that God is like the father in Jesus' story. When you are sorry for sin, God always forgives you.

- **Promise to do better.** Part of being truly sorry for sin is promising to do better.

- **Do what you can to make up for what you did.** In the Sacrament of Penance and Reconciliation, the priest gives you a penance. A **penance** is something to do or some prayers to pray to help make up for what you did wrong.

We Are Disciples

Activity Making Up

Write or talk about ways you could make up for each of these wrong choices.

Wrong Choice	Make Things Better
Fighting with a family member	
Refusing to do what your parent asks you to do	
Stealing candy from a store	

Catholic Practices

The season of Lent, when Catholics prepare for Easter, is a special time of prayerful penance.

Activity Note to God

Write a thank you note to God. Tell God how happy you are that he is always ready to welcome you back into his friendship.

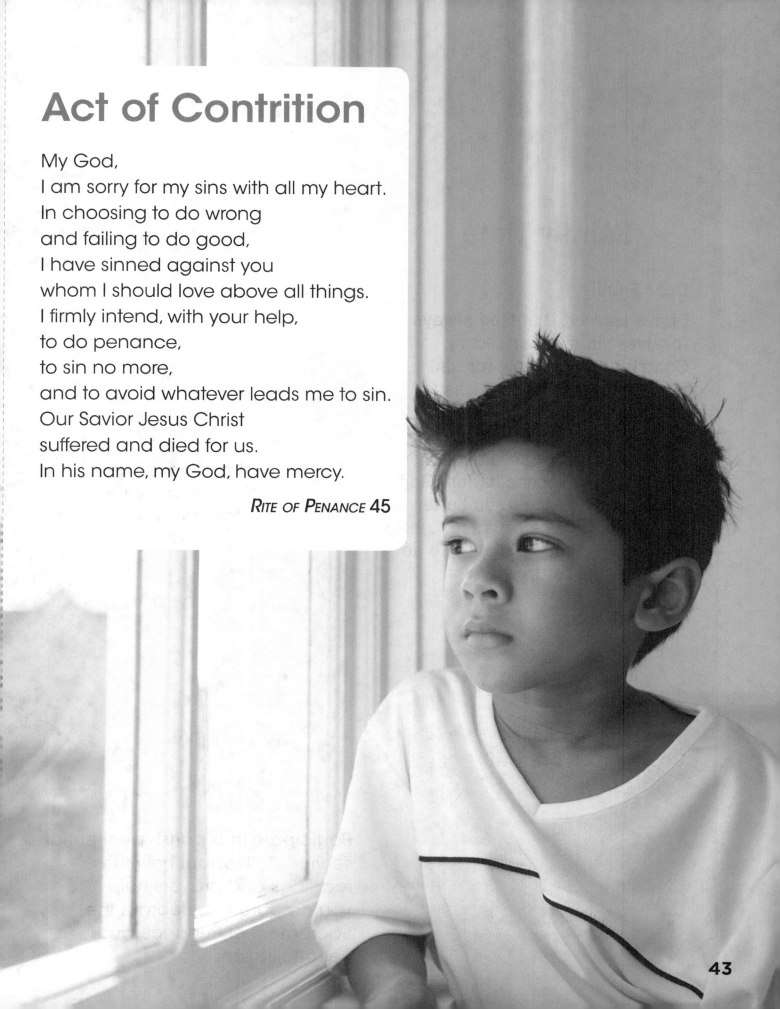

Act of Contrition

My God,
I am sorry for my sins with all my heart.
In choosing to do wrong
and failing to do good,
I have sinned against you
whom I should love above all things.
I firmly intend, with your help,
to do penance,
to sin no more,
and to avoid whatever leads me to sin.
Our Savior Jesus Christ
suffered and died for us.
In his name, my God, have mercy.

RITE OF PENANCE 45

Home and Family

Family Note

Dear Family,

I have learned that God always forgives sin if we are sorry. Contrition, or sorrow for sin, includes admitting that I have done wrong, asking God's forgiveness, and promising to do better. In the Sacrament of Penance and Reconciliation, God gives people grace to do better. The priest gives a penance to help make up for sin and to try to do better in the future.

Family Chat

Talk about ways that people in your family ask for and offer forgiveness.

On Your Own

Memorize the Act of Contrition on page 43.

With Your Family

Participate in a parish penitential service. Talk about how the readings and prayers help you prepare to celebrate the Sacrament of Penance and Reconciliation.

RCLBsacraments.com

44

Happy the sinner whose fault is removed, whose sin is forgiven. PSALM 32:1

All Better Now

Tessa was feeling cranky.

"I'm going to paint an angry picture," Tessa told her mom. She started with a big, red watercolor splotch on her paper. Tessa painted faster and faster. Suddenly, her elbow bumped the water cup. Water splashed across the table and onto Tessa's T-shirt.

Tessa started crying. "I mess everything up! I'm sorry!"

Tessa's mother hugged her. "It's all right, honey," she said. She helped Tessa clean up and change into a clean shirt. "All better now?" her mother asked.

"Yes," Tessa answered, smiling. "Thanks, Mom," she said. "Now I'm going to paint an all-better picture!"

Draw your own all-better picture. Use colors to show how you feel when someone helps you get over feeling angry or sad.

Saved!

In Luke's Gospel there are many stories about how Jesus treated people. Read the story below to see how Jesus treated a man named Zacchaeus.

Jesus was going through Jericho, where a man named Zacchaeus lived.

Zacchaeus was in charge of collecting taxes and was very rich.

Jesus was heading his way, and Zacchaeus wanted to see what he was like. But Zacchaeus was a short man and could not see over the crowd. So he ran ahead and climbed up into a sycamore tree.

When Jesus got there, he said, "Zacchaeus, hurry down! I want to stay with you today."

Zacchaeus hurried down and gladly welcomed Jesus.

Everyone who saw this started grumbling, "This man, Zacchaeus, is a sinner! And Jesus is going home to eat with him."

Later that day Zacchaeus stood up and said to the Lord, "I will give half my property to the poor. And I will now pay back four times as much to everyone I have ever cheated."

Jesus said to Zacchaeus, "Today you and your family have been saved, because you are a true son of Abraham. The Son of Man came to look for and to save people who are lost."

BASED ON LUKE 19:1–10

Let's Talk

- Why did Jesus speak to Zacchaeus?

- How did Jesus' friendship change the way Zacchaeus acted?

- How can you be closer to Jesus?

Jesus wants you to welcome him like Zacchaeus did. You can be close to Jesus when you act in loving ways. You renew your friendship with Jesus in the Sacrament of Penance and Reconciliation.

Celebrating Penance and Reconciliation

When you celebrate the Sacrament of Penance and Reconciliation, you do things in a certain order. The order is called a rite. Here is how you celebrate the Rite of Penance as an **individual penitent.** Individual means you meet privately with the priest. A penitent is someone who is sorry for having sinned.

- **The priest greets you.** You make the Sign of the Cross.

- **You share God's Word.** The priest may recite or read some words of Scripture.

- **You confess your sins to the priest.** You must always **confess** any mortal sins. Confessing venial sins can help you think about better choices in the future. Everything you confess to the priest is private.

- **The priest gives you a penance.** The priest asks you to say some prayers or gives you something to do as a penance.

- **You say a prayer of contrition.** You show that you are sorry for your sins. You promise to do better with the help of God's grace.

- **The priest gives you absolution.** Absolution means "wiping away." The sins you have committed are wiped away by God's forgiving love.

- **You are sent forth.** The priest may say, "The Lord has freed you from your sins. Go in peace."   *RITE OF PENANCE* 47

Through the Sacrament of Penance and Reconciliation, you receive the grace to help you to do better and your loving relationship with God is restored. You are also reconciled with the Body of Christ, the Church.

We Are Disciples

Activity Make a Reminder Card

On a card, write words or draw pictures that will help you remember the steps for celebrating the Sacrament of Penance and Reconciliation.

Parish Connection

Find out when your parish celebrates the Sacrament of Penance and Reconciliation.

Activity Finish the Story

With a group, act out your own ending for the story of Zacchaeus. Show what Zacchaeus does after he meets with Jesus.

What is one way Zacchaeus can make up for what he has done wrong?

How do you think people will feel about Zacchaeus now?

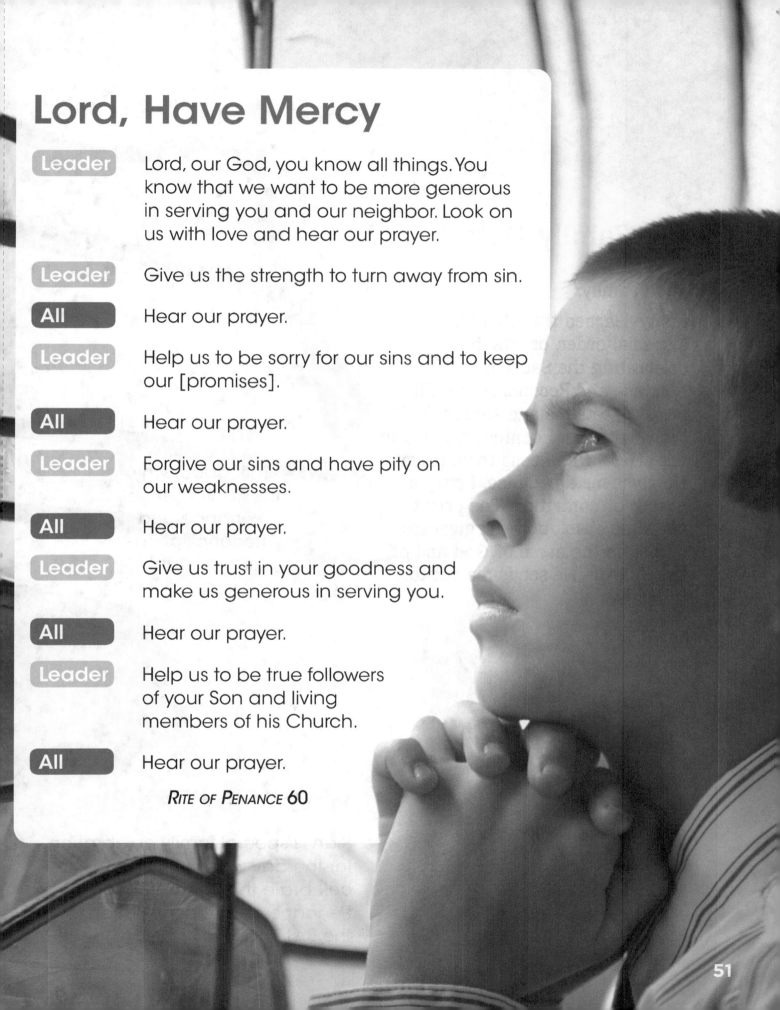

Lord, Have Mercy

Leader Lord, our God, you know all things. You know that we want to be more generous in serving you and our neighbor. Look on us with love and hear our prayer.

Leader Give us the strength to turn away from sin.

All Hear our prayer.

Leader Help us to be sorry for our sins and to keep our [promises].

All Hear our prayer.

Leader Forgive our sins and have pity on our weaknesses.

All Hear our prayer.

Leader Give us trust in your goodness and make us generous in serving you.

All Hear our prayer.

Leader Help us to be true followers of your Son and living members of his Church.

All Hear our prayer.

RITE OF PENANCE **60**

Home and Family

Family Note

Dear Family,

I have learned that there is a special order, or rite, for celebrating the Sacrament of Penance and Reconciliation. The priest greets me and shares God's Word with me. I confess my sins to the priest, who keeps them private. He gives me a penance. I pray a prayer of contrition. The priest gives me absolution—forgiveness of sin—in the name of God and of the Church. He sends me out to thank God.

Family Chat

Talk about why the Sacrament of Penance and Reconciliation is important.

On Your Own

Make up your own prayer to the Holy Spirit. Ask for help in celebrating the Sacrament of Penance and Reconciliation.

With Your Family

Plan a special family celebration for the day when you will celebrate the Sacrament of Penance and Reconciliation for the first time.

RCLBsacraments.com

Showing Love

Beloved, if God so loved us, we also must love one another. 1 JOHN 4:11

Pass It Around

I left my skateboard in the driveway again. I told my dad I was sorry, and he forgave me.

I felt so good when Dad forgave me! I cleaned my room before Mom even asked.

Mom felt so good when she didn't have to nag me about my room! She made her special enchiladas for dinner. She invited Mrs. Darcy from next door.

Mrs. Darcy felt so good about not eating dinner alone, she made us a pie! When Dad tucked me in, he told me love and forgiveness are like pieces of Mrs. Darcy's pie—you can pass them around!

> Make up your own story about how being forgiven can start a whole chain of good feelings. Tell or act out your story.

Great Love

Read this story from the Bible to find out how Jesus made someone feel good. What do you think will happen as a result?

A Pharisee (named Simon) invited Jesus to have dinner with him. So Jesus went to the Pharisee's home and got ready to eat.

When a sinful woman in that town found out Jesus was there, she bought an expensive bottle of perfume. Then she came and stood behind Jesus. She cried and started washing his feet with her tears and drying them with her hair. The woman kissed his feet and poured perfume on them.

The Pharisee who invited Jesus saw this and said to himself, "If this man were really a prophet, he would know what kind of woman is touching him! He would know she was a sinner!"

Jesus turned toward the woman and said to Simon, "Have you noticed this woman? When I came into your home, you didn't give me any water so I could wash my feet. But she has washed my feet with her tears and dried them with her hair.

"You didn't greet me with a kiss, but from the time I came in, she has not stopped kissing my feet.

"You didn't even pour olive oil on my head, but she has poured expensive perfume on my feet.

"So I tell you that all her sins are forgiven, and that is why she has shown great love."

BASED ON LUKE 7:36–39, 44–47

Let's Talk

■ What did the Pharisee think about the woman who came to see Jesus?

■ What signs of love did the woman show to Jesus?

■ According to Jesus, why did the woman show such great love?

Jesus forgave the woman's sins. How do you think she felt when he did that? How do you think the woman might change as a result of Jesus' kindness?

Love and Grace

The Sacrament of Penance and Reconciliation brings you back to friendship with God. You come back home to your Church family. Your sins are forgiven. You grow in love and grace.

God's forgiveness makes you feel better. When you are forgiven, it's easier to forgive others. When you know you are loved, it's easier to show love to others.

In Penance and Reconciliation you go through conversion. **Conversion** means "turning around." You turn away from sin. You turn toward God's love. You turn away from bad habits. You turn toward good actions and choices.

Growing in Love

The Sacrament of Penance and Reconciliation does not end when you leave the reconciliation room or the church. You do the penance the priest has given you. You do what you can to make up for any wrong you have done. God's gift of grace stays with you. The Holy Spirit helps you grow in love.

Do you practice a sport or a musical instrument? Celebrating the Sacrament of Penance and Reconciliation is like practicing for a life of goodness. You learn good habits, like patience and kindness. These good habits are called **virtues.** Like the woman who showed signs of love to Jesus, you share God's love and mercy with everyone you meet.

Activity

With your teacher's help, create a group list of virtues. **Tell how you can practice these good habits at home and in school.**

We Are Disciples

Activity The Reconciliation Tree

On the apples, write or draw good things that come from celebrating the Sacrament of Penance and Reconciliation.

Catholic Practices

Catholics must be absolved from mortal sin before receiving Holy Communion.

Activity Make a Bookmark

On one side of a card write, "I Am Forgiven." On the other side of the card write, "I Forgive." Decorate the card. Use it as a bookmark to remind yourself that being forgiven and forgiving others are as closely connected as the two sides of the card.

A New Heart

Leader Merciful God,
touch our hearts
and convert us to yourself.

Leader Where sin has divided and
scattered us,

All May your love make us one again.

Leader Where sin has brought weakness,

All May your power bring healing
and strength.

Leader Where sin has brought death,

All May your Spirit raise us to new life.

Leader Give us a new heart to love you, so that
our lives might teach everyone about
Jesus, your Son.

All Amen.

ADAPTED FROM *RITE OF PENANCE* 99

Home and Family

Family Note

Dear Family,

I have learned that the Sacrament of Penance and Reconciliation is about conversion—turning away from sin and toward God's love. Celebrating the Sacrament of Penance and Reconciliation helps people grow in love, be more forgiving of others, and practice virtues, or good habits. God's grace strengthens people to make better choices and be more loving.

Family Chat

Talk about times when being forgiven made you want to be forgiving.

On Your Own

Think of three people who could use your forgiveness or a sign of love from you. Plan how you can let these people know that you forgive them, or share a sign of love with them.

With Your Family

Make a list of virtues, or habits of goodness, that your family needs to practice. (Examples include patience, kindness, forgiveness and generosity.) Make refrigerator magnets with the names of virtues on them to use as reminders.

RCLBsacraments.com

Living Reconciliation

> When he saw their faith, he said, "As for you, your sins are forgiven."
>
> LUKE 5:20

Forgiveness

Forgiveness is a wonderful gift! You have received this special and holy gift in the Sacrament of Penance and Reconciliation. By the power of the Holy Spirit, you received God's grace, love, and forgiveness.

In this session, you will look back on your celebration of the Sacrament of Penance and Reconciliation. We will talk about what happened, how you felt, and what it means. Remember some of the things you did to prepare for the Sacrament of Penance and Reconciliation.

- My favorite part of preparing for the Sacrament of Penance and Reconciliation was...

- I heard many Bible stories about how Jesus forgave people. One that I remember is...

We Remember

When you receive a Sacrament, you are part of a holy mystery. A mystery is something so full of meaning we cannot completely understand it. A Sacrament is a mystery. The Holy Trinity is a mystery.

Now that you have received the Sacrament of Penance and Reconciliation, you have experienced the power of God's forgiving love.

Think again about the different parts of the celebration. As you recall each part, tell why each is important. This will give you a deeper understanding of the Sacrament.

The Sacrament of Penance and Reconciliation is a community celebration. You, your family, the Church, and the angels of God all celebrate because you have been forgiven. Go back in your mind and heart to the day of the celebration of First Penance and Reconciliation.

Gathering

What was it like when you arrived at church to celebrate the Sacrament? Who was with you? What did you do? How were you feeling?

Write or draw what you remember.

Word of God

You hear a story from the Bible that calls you to repent and change your heart.

Picture yourself as you sat and listened to God's Word being proclaimed. What do you remember?

Examination of Conscience

Before celebrating the Sacrament, you think about your actions and attitudes that need to change. You feel sorry for wrong choices.

What will be the hardest thing for you to change?

Confession of Sins

Naming your sins helps you to admit you are wrong and want to change.

What do you remember feeling as you were sitting and talking to the priest?

Contrition

You say you are sorry for your sins. Admitting your sin and showing you are truly sorry helps you on the path to **conversion.**

What are some things you want to change in your life?

Penance

The priest gives you a good deed to do or a prayer to pray. Accepting your penance is a way of showing you are sorry and that you want to live in a new way.

What things can you continue to do to become a better person?

Absolution

When the priest raised his hand and you heard the words, "I absolve you from your sins in the name of the Father, and of the Son, and of the Holy Spirit," how did you feel?

When you went back to your place, what do you remember thinking?

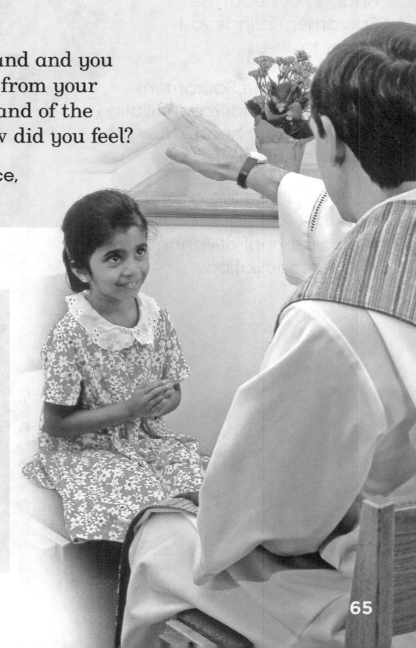

Blessing and Dismissal

You are sent forth in peace with a new heart to live in a new way.

At the very end of the celebration, what were you feeling? What did you and your family do after you left the church?

A New Beginning

The Sacrament of Penance and Reconciliation is a new beginning! With your sins forgiven and your heart made new, you go forth to live as Jesus calls you to live. The Sacrament is part of your conversion, your change of heart. The Sacrament brings you closer to Jesus.

How has the Sacrament of Penance and Reconciliation changed your heart? How are you different?

How will you live differently now that you have received the Sacrament of Penance and Reconciliation?

Doing the Work of Jesus

And all this is from God, who has reconciled us to himself through Christ and given us the ministry of reconciliation, . . . So we are ambassadors for Christ. 2 Corinthians 5:18, 20a

Leader After receiving the Sacrament of Penance and Reconciliation, Jesus asks us to go forth and help others be reconciled. We are to show others what it means to be good disciples who forgive others. We are to help others ask for forgiveness. When we go forth and do what Jesus commands, we are being ambassadors of Christ. An ambassador is one who goes forth to represent another person or group.

Sit silently and imagine being an ambassador for Christ as I read the story from the Bible.

(Read 2 Corinthians 5:17–21)

Reflection How does celebrating the Sacrament of Penance and Reconciliation help you to be an ambassador for Jesus Christ? What will you do? Give an example.

Leader Together let us pray:

All Dear God, thank you for the gift of reconciliation. Help me to follow your Son, Jesus, more closely. May I be an ambassador of your gift of mercy. I ask this through Christ, our Lord. Amen.

Home and Family

Family Note

Dear Family,

I have learned that the Sacrament of Penance and Reconciliation is a great gift. It is a gift of grace and forgiveness. I am an ambassador of reconciliation. I'll bring forgiveness and mercy to others.

Family Chat

How can our family be ambassadors of reconciliation?

On Your Own

Think about the penance the priest gave you during the celebration of the Sacrament. Have you done it? Is there more you could do? Go be an ambassador of reconciliation!

With Your Family

Talk about times when various family members have celebrated the Sacrament of Penance and Reconciliation. What meaning did it have? Have adults tell what it was like when they were young. Remember to discuss penitential services you have celebrated or will celebrate in the future!

 RCLBsacraments.com

a Little Catechism

Then he took the bread, said the blessing, broke it,
and gave it to them, saying, "This is my body,
which will be given for you; do this in memory of me."

LUKE 22: 19

We Believe

We Celebrate

We Live

We Pray

We Believe

It is important to have the right words to talk about your faith. When you use the right words, you can share your faith with others. Here is a list of some of the things you have learned. As you grow older, you will learn more and more about these beliefs.

1. **The Blessed Trinity** is Three Persons in One God: God the Father, God the Son, and God the Holy Spirit. There is only One God, but God is Three Persons. You can say, "I believe in God—Father, Son, and Holy Spirit."

2. **Jesus is the Son of God,** the only Son of the Father. God loved his people so much that he sent his Son, Jesus, to die for our sins. Jesus became man and came to Earth to show us the Father's love and to save all people.

3. **The name Jesus** means "God saves." Jesus saved us by his Passion, Death, Resurrection, and Ascension. This is called the Paschal Mystery.

4. **The Paschal Mystery,** Jesus' Passion, Death, Resurrection, and Ascension, is made present in the celebration of the Eucharist. Its saving effects are carried on through the Sacraments of the Church.

5. **Jesus will come again** at the end of time to judge those living and those who have died.

6. **God made us** to love him, and it is only with God that we will find true happiness.

7. **The gift of the Holy Spirit** was given to the Church. The Holy Spirit works with the Father and the Son to guide the Church.

8. **The Apostles** taught the people all that Jesus had taught them. The Church carries on the work of Jesus today with the help of the Holy Spirit.

9. **The Church** is the People of God, the Body of Christ. Those nourished by the Body of Christ become the Body of Christ. The Church shares the Good News of Jesus Christ with others.

10. **The Church teaches** the Law of God. Catholics follow the teachings of the Church, especially the teachings of the Pope, and the bishops together with the Pope.

11. **The Holy Spirit** guides the Church and helps keep the followers of Jesus faithful to the truth. The Church is the Temple of the Holy Spirit.

12. **Those who follow Jesus** know that they are called to serve one another in love and to share the message of Jesus with others.

13. **Jesus gives many gifts** and the best gift is a share in God's own life, which is called grace.

14. **The Risen Jesus** is with the People of God in the Eucharist and in the other Sacraments.

15. **God created us.** Our lives are good. Every gift we have comes from God. We are free and can make choices.

16. **In Baptism** we become adopted children of God through his Son, Jesus Christ.

17. **God** has given every person the gift of free will. This freedom makes people responsible for the choices they make.

18. **We respond** to God's love by keeping his Commandments and by trying with all our hearts to be faithful, to respect all life, and to do what is right.

19. **Mary is the Mother of God** and our Mother, too. We turn to Mary in prayer. She will help us.

20. **Prayer** is lifting one's mind and heart to God. In prayer we praise God, ask God to help us, and give thanks to God for his gifts. We also pray for other people. Prayer is the best way to stay on the right path.

Important Questions

The questions and answers below will help you remember what you learn as you prepare for the Sacraments of Penance and Reconciliation and Eucharist. Try to learn the answers by heart.

1. Why are the Gospels so important?

The four Gospels are important because they tell about Jesus Christ—his life and his teachings.

2. What is a conscience?

A conscience is the ability to know what is right and to do what is right. God's Law and the teaching of the Church help to form a correct conscience.

3. How does sin affect a person's relationship with God?

Sin is an offense against God and his Law. Sin is choosing to turn away from God. Mortal sin breaks a person's relationship with God.

4. Which Sacrament helps people heal their relationship with God?

The Sacrament of Penance and Reconciliation celebrates God's loving forgiveness.

5. Why is the Eucharist the heart of Catholic life?

The night before he died Jesus gave us the Eucharist by sharing himself, Body and Blood, under the appearance of bread and wine. Jesus continues to be present today in the Mass: in the people gathered; in the Word of God; in the person of the priest; and especially in the consecrated bread and wine which have become the Body and Blood of Christ.

6. What mission do you receive at the end of Mass?

I am sent to glorify the Lord by my life.

Things to Remember

The Gifts of the Holy Spirit

- Wisdom
- Understanding
- Knowledge
- Counsel
- Piety
- Fortitude
- Fear of the Lord

Spiritual Works of Mercy

- Help the sinner.
- Teach the ignorant.
- Counsel the doubtful.
- Comfort the sorrowful.
- Bear wrongs patiently.
- Forgive injuries.
- Pray for the living and the dead.

Corporal Works of Mercy

- Feed the hungry.
- Give drink to the thirsty.
- Clothe the naked.
- Shelter the homeless.
- Visit the sick.
- Visit the imprisoned.
- Bury the dead.

The Great Commandment

You shall love the Lord, your God, with all your heart, with all your soul, and with all your mind.

You shall love your neighbor as yourself.

We Celebrate

Sacraments

The Seven Sacraments are outward signs and celebrations of God's love and life, or grace. The Sacraments communicate and share God's life as the gift of grace. Through the Sacraments you give worship and praise to God, grow in holiness, work to build up God's reign on Earth, and strengthen the unity of God's people.

Christian initiation happens in three Sacraments together: Baptism, which is the beginning of new life in Christ; Confirmation, which is its strengthening; and Eucharist, which nourishes you with Christ's Body and Blood to become more like Jesus. Penance and Reconciliation and the Anointing of the Sick are the Sacraments of Healing. Holy Orders and Matrimony are the Sacraments at the Service of Communion.

Baptism

You are freed from Original Sin and from all sin. You are given the new life of grace by which you become an adopted child of God, one with Christ in the Holy Spirit, and a member of the Church. Baptism imprints a spiritual mark on your soul that claims you for Christ. Baptism can only be received once.

Confirmation

The gift of the Holy Spirit strengthens you to live as Jesus did. As in Baptism, your soul is imprinted with a spiritual mark as a sign of the Holy Spirit's presence. The Holy Spirit will help you by word and action to witness to Christ.

Eucharist

In Eucharist Christ is truly present in the consecrated bread and wine. To receive Holy Communion you must be in the state of grace. You are encouraged to receive Holy Communion every time you go to Mass.

Penance and Reconciliation

When you are sorry for your sins, God offers you pardon and peace through the words and actions of a priest.

Anointing of the Sick

A priest anoints a person who is sick or elderly and offers God's healing comfort and forgiveness.

Holy Orders

The Church ordains deacons, priests, and bishops to teach, to lead, to celebrate, to guide, and to serve the People of God.

Matrimony

A man and a woman promise to live their whole lives as husband and wife, and become a sign of God's love.

The Celebration of the Eucharist

When the hour came, [Jesus] took his place at table with the apostles. He said to them, "I have eagerly [wanted] to eat this Passover with you before I suffer for, I tell you, I shall not eat it [again] until there is fulfillment in the kingdom of God."

Then [Jesus] took the bread, said the blessing, broke it, and gave it to them, saying, "This is my body, which will be given for you; do this in memory of me." [In the same way, he took] the cup after they had eaten, saying, "This cup is the new covenant in my blood, which will be shed for you." LUKE 22:14-16, 19-20

At Mass, followers of Jesus all around the world come to worship and praise God, and to remember the actions of Jesus at the Last Supper. They listen to and learn from the reading of God's living Word.

They remember and relive the great love of Jesus, who gave up his life for all people. They share in that love by receiving the Body and Blood of Christ in Holy Communion. Finally, they go to their homes in peace, knowing that they are called to glorify the Lord by their lives.

Introductory Rites

At the beginning of Mass, the People of God are gathered with Christ and with one another. We prepare to worship God.

Entrance Procession

We stand as the priest and other ministers process into the assembly. We join in singing an entrance song.

Greeting

Priest: In the name of the Father, and of the Son, and of the Holy Spirit.

People: Amen.

Priest: The grace of our Lord Jesus Christ, and the love of God, and the communion of the Holy Spirit be with you all.

People: And with your spirit.

Penitential Act

We praise God for his mercy.

Priest: Lord, have mercy.
People: Lord, have mercy.

Priest: Christ, have mercy.
People: Christ, have mercy.

Priest: Lord, have mercy.
People: Lord, have mercy.

Gloria

On most Sundays we pray the Gloria,
a hymn of praise.

**Glory to God in the highest,
and on earth peace to people of good will.**

**We praise you, we bless you,
we adore you, we glorify you,
we give thanks for your great glory,
Lord God, heavenly King,
O God, almighty Father.**

**Lord Jesus Christ, Only Begotten Son,
Lord God, Lamb of God, Son of the Father,
you take away the sins of the world,
    have mercy on us;
you take away the sins of the world,
    receive our prayer;
you are seated at the right hand of the Father,
    have mercy on us.**

**For you alone are the Holy One,
you alone are the Lord,
you alone are the Most High,
Jesus Christ,
with the Holy Spirit,
in the glory of God the Father.**

Amen.

Collect

We observe a moment of silence and lift up
our hearts and minds to God. The priest
leads us in prayer.

Priest: Let us pray.
People: Amen.

Liturgy of the Word

We listen to the Word of God.

First Reading

This reading is taken from the Old Testament or, during the Easter season, from the Acts of the Apostles. At the end of the reading the lector says:

Lector: The word of the Lord.

People: Thanks be to God.

Responsorial Psalm

The cantor leads us in singing a psalm.

Second Reading

The Second Reading is taken from the letters in the New Testament or from the Acts of the Apostles. At the end of the reading the lector says:

Lector: The word of the Lord.

People: Thanks be to God.

Alleluia or Gospel Acclamation

As we sing the Alleluia we show reverence for Jesus, the Word of God. We stand to show that we believe Jesus is with us in the Gospel. During Lent we do not sing the Alleluia. We sing a different acclamation.

Gospel

Priest or deacon:
          The Lord be with you.

People: And with your spirit.

Priest or deacon:
          A reading from the holy Gospel according to (name of the Gospel writer).

People: Glory to you, O Lord.

Priest or deacon (at the end of the Gospel):
          The Gospel of the Lord.

People: Praise to you, Lord Jesus Christ.

Homily

The priest or deacon helps the community to understand and live the Scripture that has been proclaimed.

Profession of Faith

We stand and profess our faith. We usually pray the Nicene Creed (see page 89). When we pray the creed we are saying what we believe.

Prayer of the Faithful

We pray for the needs of the Church, for public leaders, for the Salvation of the world, and for the needs of people. After each petition we might respond:

People: Lord, hear our prayer.

Liturgy of the Eucharist

We give thanks and praise.

Preparation of the Altar and Gifts

We sit as the gifts of bread and wine are brought up and the altar is prepared.

The priest lifts up the bread and says:

Priest: Blessed are you,
        Lord God of all creation,
        for through your goodness
          we have received
        the bread we offer you:
        fruit of the earth and
          work of human hands,
        it will become for us the bread of life.

People: Blessed be God for ever.

The priest lifts up the chalice of wine and prays:

Priest: Blessed are you,
        Lord God of all creation.
        for through your goodness
          we have received
        the wine we offer you:
        fruit of the vine and
          work of human hands,
        it will become our spiritual drink.

People: Blessed be God for ever.

Priest: Pray, brethren (brothers and sisters),
        that my sacrifice and yours
        may be acceptable to God,
        the almighty Father.

We stand to say the following prayer.

**People: May the Lord accept the sacrifice
        at your hands
        for the praise and glory of his name,
        for our good
        and the good of all his holy Church.**

Prayer over the Offerings

The priest says the Prayer over the Offerings.

People: Amen.

Eucharistic Prayer

The priest invites us to give thanks and praise.

Priest: The Lord be with you.

People: And with your spirit.

Priest: Lift up your hearts.

People: We lift them up to the Lord.

Priest: Let us give thanks to the Lord our God.

People: It is right and just.

After the priest says the Preface, a prayer that gives a special reason for praising God, we join in saying or singing the acclamation.

**All: Holy, Holy, Holy Lord God
        of hosts.
        Heaven and earth are full
        of your glory.
        Hosanna in the highest.
        Blessed is he who comes
        in the name of the Lord.
        Hosanna in the highest.**

The "Holy, Holy, Holy" is followed by a prayer asking that the power of the Holy Spirit might come upon the gifts and make them holy, that is, become the Body and Blood of Christ, and that those who receive these gifts might be gathered into one by the Holy Spirit.

At the consecration the bread and wine become the Body and Blood of the Lord through the power of the Holy Spirit and the words of the priest. Jesus is truly present in the bread and wine that we receive at Communion.

After the consecration, we pray or sing the Memorial Acclamation.

Priest: The mystery of faith.

**People: We proclaim your Death, O Lord,
           and profess your Resurrection
           until you come again.**

The priest prays for the Church and for the living and the dead and that one day we will live in Heaven. The doxology concludes the Eucharistic Prayer.

Priest: Through him, and with him, and in him,
           O God, almighty Father,
           in the unity of the Holy Spirit,
           all glory and honor is yours,
           for ever and ever.

People: Amen.

The Eucharistic Prayer ends with a great "Amen," a "so be it" or a "yes" to all of the Eucharistic Prayers that we make our own.

Communion Rite

The Lord's Prayer

As we prepare ourselves to receive the Body and Blood of the Lord, we are invited to say the Lord's Prayer (see page 88).

Sign of Peace

We pray for peace and unity for the Church and the whole world.

Priest or deacon:
        The peace of the Lord be with
        you always.

People: And with your spirit.

Priest or deacon:
        Let us offer each other the sign
        of peace.

Breaking of the Bread

At the Last Supper, Jesus broke the bread and gave it to his disciples. The priest breaks the consecrated host so it can be shared. While he is breaking the host, we say or sing:

**Lamb of God, you take away the sins
    of the world,
have mercy on us.**

**Lamb of God, you take away the sins
    of the world,
have mercy on us.**

**Lamb of God, you take away the sins
    of the world,
grant us peace.**

Communion

The priest raises the consecrated host and proclaims:

Priest: Behold the Lamb of God,
behold him who takes away the sins of the world.
Blessed are those called to the supper of the Lamb.

**People: Lord, I am not worthy
that you should enter under my roof,
but only say the word
and my soul shall be healed.**

The priest receives Holy Communion.
We process up the aisle to receive the Body and Blood of Christ.

Priest, deacon, or Eucharist minister:
The Body of Christ.

People: Amen.

We receive the consecrated host in our hand or on our tongue.

Priest, deacon, or Eucharist minister:
The Blood of Christ.

People: Amen.

We take a sip from the cup.

Prayer after Communion

We stand as the priest leads us in prayer.

Priest: Let us pray.
People: Amen.

Concluding Rites

Priest: The Lord be with you.
People: And with your spirit.

Blessing

Priest: May almighty God bless you, the Father, and the Son, and the Holy Spirit.
People: Amen.

Dismissal

At the conclusion of Mass we are sent out to help others as Jesus did.

Priest or deacon:
Go and announce the Gospel of the Lord.

People: Thanks be to God.

The priest kisses the altar as a sign of reverence. He and the other ministers process out of the church while we sing a concluding hymn.

Eucharist

- Eucharist is at the heart of the life of the Church.

- The consecrated bread and wine are truly the Body and Blood of Christ.

- Jesus gave us the Eucharist at his Last Supper.

- In order to receive Holy Communion worthily, you must be free from mortal sin.

- Catholics are encouraged to receive Eucharist every time they go to Mass. Catholics are required to receive Eucharist at least once a year during the Easter season.

- Catholics fast from food and drink (except water or medicine) for one hour before receiving Holy Communion.

How to Receive Eucharist

There are different ways to receive Holy Communion—in your hand, on your tongue, and from the cup.

If you choose to receive Holy Communion in your hand:

- Bow, hold out both hands, palms up, with one hand resting on top of the other.
- The priest, deacon, or Eucharistic minister says, "The Body of Christ," and places the consecrated host in your hand. You answer, **"Amen."**
- Step to one side. Using the hand that is underneath, take the host in your fingers and place it in your mouth. Swallow the consecrated host.

If you choose to receive Holy Communion on your tongue:

- Fold your hands in prayer. Bow.
- The priest, deacon, or Eucharistic minister says, "The Body of Christ." You answer **"Amen."**
- Open your mouth and put your tongue out to receive the host. Swallow the consecrated host.

You may also receive the Blood of Christ from the cup.

- After you have received the Body of Christ, go to the priest, deacon, or Eucharistic minister who is offering the cup.
- The priest, deacon, or Eucharistic minister will say, "The Blood of Christ." You answer, **"Amen."**
- Take the cup of consecrated wine in both hands and take a small sip. Return the cup to the minister.

After receiving Communion, return to your place and kneel or stand. Join in singing the Communion hymn. After everyone has received Communion, and after the Communion hymn is finished, kneel or sit quietly for a few minutes, giving thanks to God.

Penance and Reconciliation

There are two ways we can celebrate the Sacrament of Penance and Reconciliation—individually or communally.

The following are the steps for individual confession.

1. **Greeting**
   - The priest greets us and we make the Sign of the Cross.
   - The priest may say these or similar words:

     May God, who has enlightened every heart, help you to know your sins and trust in his mercy. Amen.

2. **Reading of the Word of God**

   The priest may read a passage from the Bible.

3. **Confession of Sins and Acceptance of Penance**
   - We tell our sins to the priest. We must confess mortal sins. We may also confess venial sins.
   - After we confess our sins, the priest may talk to us and advise us. Then he gives us our penance. A penance is something we do to show we are sorry and that we want to make up for our sins.

4. **Prayer of the Penitent and Absolution**
   - The priest asks us to pray the Act of Contrition to say we are sorry for our sins.

   - The priest gives absolution by extending his hands over our head and saying:

     God, the Father of mercies,
     through the death and Resurrection
        of his Son
     has reconciled the world to himself
     and sent the Holy Spirit among us
     for the forgiveness of sins;
     through the ministry of the Church
     may God give you pardon and
        peace,

     The priest makes the Sign of the Cross over our head as he says:
     and I absolve you from your sins
     in the name of the Father,
     and of the Son,
     and of the Holy Spirit.

   - We make the Sign of the Cross and say, **"Amen."**

5. **Proclamation of Praise of God and Dismissal**
   - After the absolution, the priest continues: Give thanks to the Lord, for he is good.
   - We respond: **His mercy endures for ever.**
   - The priest sends us forth saying: The Lord has freed you from your sins. Go in peace.

We Live

God's Law

Sometimes it can be hard to choose the right thing to do. Rules can help you to stay on the right track. Good rules can help you take care of yourself—inside and out. Rules help everyone make choices that lead to happier and healthier lives.

Good Advice

Follow the advice below to avoid temptations and make good choices.

F igure out your choices.

R est your brain awhile, and pray.

E ase off—don't decide in a hurry.

S top and think about the consequences.

H old off until you are pretty sure.

S et your conscience into action.

T ake it slow and easy.

A sk what Jesus would do.

R eview all the facts and advice.

T hen make a right choice.

The Ten Commandments

These are ten rules for being faithful to God. Following the Commandments provides a clear path for you. The Ten Commandments help you live out your covenant relationship with God.

1. I am the LORD, your God. You shall not have other gods besides me.

2. You shall not take the name of the LORD, your God, in vain.

3. Remember to keep holy the Sabbath day (LORD's Day).

4. Honor your father and your mother.

5. You shall not kill.

6. You shall not commit adultery.

7. You shall not steal.

8. You shall not bear false witness against your neighbor.

9. You shall not covet your neighbor's wife.

10. You shall not covet anything that belongs to your neighbor.

The Precepts of the Church

The Church has rules that help us live the Gospel. They tell Catholics how to show love for God and for others.

1. You shall attend Mass on Sundays and on holy days of obligation. Do no unnecessary work on Sunday.

2. Receive the Sacrament of Penance and Reconciliation once a year.

3. Receive the Eucharist (Holy Communion) at least once during the Easter season.

4. Do penance (fasting and abstinence) on the appointed days.

5. Contribute to the support of the Church.

The Beatitudes

Jesus used the Beatitudes to teach people what is truly important in God's kingdom. The Beatitudes show people how they should live and what they should treasure in order to be happy with God now and forever.

Blessed are the poor in spirit,
for theirs is the kingdom of heaven.
Blessed are they who mourn,
for they will be comforted.
Blessed are the meek,
for they will inherit the land.
Blessed are they who hunger
and thirst for righteousness,
for they will be satisfied.

Blessed are the merciful,
for they will be shown mercy.
Blessed are the clean of heart,
for they will see God.
Blessed are the peacemakers,
for they will be called children of God.
Blessed are they who are persecuted for
the sake of righteousness,
for theirs is the kingdom of heaven.

MATTHEW 5:3–10

Things to Know

1. What is sin?

Sin is making a choice to do something wrong. In sin we turn our hearts away from God's love. Sin not only hurts our relationship with God, but with one another.

There are two kinds of sin: venial and mortal.

- A venial sin is a lesser sin. It is when a person is not being as good a friend to God and to people as God wants.
- A mortal sin is a serious sin. The person completely breaks off his or her friendship with God. Mortal sin must be confessed in the Sacrament of Penance and Reconciliation.

2. What is necessary for something to be a mortal sin?

Something is a mortal sin if the act is seriously wrong, the person knows it is seriously wrong, and the person chooses to do it anyway.

3. Ask for forgiveness.

- When you have done something wrong, ask God to forgive you.
- If you have committed a serious sin, celebrate the Sacrament of Penance and Reconciliation.

An Examination of Conscience

You examine your conscience to help you live as a child of God.
You ask yourself if you are living as Jesus wants you to live.
You ask for the help of the Holy Spirit to be more like Jesus.
Ask yourself how you act toward:

God

Do I talk to God every day?

Do I say God's name only in a prayerful way?

Have I missed Mass on Sunday through my own fault?

Am I trying to trust God like Jesus did?

Myself

Do I do things that will help me grow as God wants?

Do I take care of what I have?

Do I care for the things of the earth?

Do I thank God for the gifts and talents God has given me?

My Family, My Friends, and Other People

Do I do my chores well, or do I have to be asked?

Do I try to do my best at school?

Do I obey my parents and show them respect?

When someone who is taking care of me asks me to do something good, do I obey?

Am I generous? Do I share what I have with others, especially those in need?

When I am angry, do I talk about it, or do I say or do things to hurt whoever hurt me?

Do I say I'm sorry to the person I have hurt, and I forgive you to the person who has hurt me?

Do I play fair, or do I ever cheat at school, work, or games?

Have I taken something that doesn't belong to me?

Do I tell the whole truth or do I let people believe something that isn't true?

Am I jealous of what other people have?

We Pray

Sign of the Cross

In the name of the Father,
and of the Son,
and of the Holy Spirit. Amen.

Our Father

Our Father, who art in heaven,
hallowed be thy name;
thy kingdom come,
thy will be done
    on earth as it is in heaven.
Give us this day our daily bread,
and forgive us our trespasses,
as we forgive those who trespass
    against us;
and lead us not into temptation,
    but deliver us from evil.
Amen.

The Hail Mary

Hail, Mary, full of grace,
the Lord is with thee.
Blessed art thou among women
and blessed is the fruit
    of thy womb, Jesus.
Holy Mary, Mother of God,
pray for us sinners,
now and at the hour of our death.
Amen.

Glory Be (Doxology)

Glory be to the Father
and to the Son
and to the Holy Spirit,
as it was in the beginning
is now, and ever shall be
world without end. Amen.

Act of Contrition

My God,
I am sorry for my sins with all my heart.
In choosing to do wrong and failing
    to do good,
I have sinned against you,
whom I should love above all things.
I firmly intend, with your help,
to do penance, to sin no more,
and to avoid whatever leads me to sin.
Our Savior Jesus Christ
suffered and died for us.
In his name, my God, have mercy.
Amen.

Nicene Creed

I believe in one God,
the Father almighty,
maker of heaven and earth,
of all things visible and invisible.

I believe in one Lord Jesus Christ,
the Only Begotten Son of God,
born of the Father before all ages.
God from God, Light from Light,
true God from true God,
begotten, not made,
    consubstantial with the Father;
through him all things were made.
For us men and for our salvation
he came down from heaven,
and by the Holy Spirit was incarnate
    of the Virgin Mary,
and became man.

For our sake he was crucified under
    Pontius Pilate,
he suffered death and was buried,
and rose again on the third day
in accordance with the Scriptures.
He ascended into heaven
and is seated at the right hand of the Father.
He will come again in glory
to judge the living and the dead
and his kingdom will have no end.

I believe in the Holy Spirit, the Lord,
    the giver of life,
who proceeds from the Father and the Son,
who with the Father and the Son is adored
    and glorified,
who has spoken through the prophets.

I believe in one, holy, catholic and
    apostolic Church.
I confess one Baptism for the forgiveness
    of sins
and I look forward to the resurrection
    of the dead
and the life of the world to come. Amen.

Confiteor (Penitential Act)

I confess to almighty God
and to you, my brothers and sisters,
that I have greatly sinned,
in my thoughts and in my words,
in what I have done and in what I have
    failed to do,
through my fault, through my fault,
through my most grievous fault;
therefore I ask blessed Mary ever-Virgin,
all the Angels and Saints,
and you, my brothers and sisters,
to pray for me to the Lord our God.

Glossary

absolution The prayer in the Sacrament of Penance and Reconciliation in which the priest, by the power given to the Church by Christ, forgives the sinner.

Baptism Frees us from Original Sin and all sin and welcomes us to the People of God, the Church.

confess To admit that we have done something wrong. In Penance and Reconciliation we confess or tell our sins to a priest.

conscience A gift from God that helps us know right from wrong. It helps us move toward good and avoid evil.

contrition To be truly sorry for our sins and to resolve to sin no more.

conversion Turning away from sin and living as a child of God.

covenant God's holy promise to be with his people always.

eternal life Living forever with God in the happiness of Heaven.

examination of conscience We carefully look at our words and actions to see if we are living as children of God. We ask the Holy Spirit for help in recognizing our wrongdoing.

free will God's gift that allows us the freedom to choose between good and evil.

grace God's own life within us. The word grace means "gift." Grace helps us follow Jesus more closely.

Great Commandment You shall love the Lord, your God, with all your heart, and with all your soul, and with all your mind. You shall love your neighbor as yourself.

mercy The loving kindness that God shows us.

mortal sin A serious failure to love and respect God, oneself, and others. For a sin to be mortal: it must be serious; we must know it is serious, and we freely choose to do it anyway. A mortal sin separates us from God. We must confess mortal sins before receiving Communion.

Original Sin The sin of the first humans that is passed on to all generations. Human nature was wounded by the first sin and is deprived of original holiness and justice. Original Sin also describes the pull everyone feels toward doing things that are wrong.

penance A step in the Sacrament when we promise to do something that shows we are truly sorry.

Penance and Reconciliation The Sacrament for the forgiveness of sin, it welcomes a person back to friendship with God and the Church.

penitent A person who is sorry for having sinned.

satisfaction A way of making up for our sins, like doing the penance that the priest gives us in Penance and Reconciliation.

sin Choosing to do what is wrong, rather than showing love the way God wants.

social sin When a whole a group of people chooses not to show love.

Ten Commandments The Laws God gave to Moses to help people grow in holiness and love.

venial sin Choosing to do something we know is wrong. Venial sins weaken our friendship with God.

virtue A habit to do the good, like patience and kindness.

Music Lyrics

Psalm 100—Nosotros Somos Su Pueblo/We Are God's People

Refrain

Nosotros somos su pueblo.
We are God's people.
Y ovejas de su rebaño.
The flock of the Lord.

1. Make a joyful noise to the Lord,
   all the earth.
   Worship the Lord with gladness;
   come into the presence of the Lord
   with singing.

2. Know that the Lord is God,
   our maker to whom we belong.
   We are the people of God,
   the flock of the Lord.

Christ, Be Our Light

Refrain

Christ, be our light!
Shine in our hearts.
Shine through the darkness.
Christ, be our light!
Shine in your church gathered today.

1. Longing for light, we wait in darkness.
   Longing for truth, we turn to you.
   Make us your own, your holy people,
   light for the world to see.

3. Longing for food, many are hungry.
   Longing for water, many still thirst.
   Make us your bread, broken for others,
   shared until all are fed.

5. Many the gifts, many the people,
   Many the hearts that yearn to belong.
   Let us be servants to one another,
   making your kingdom come.

Change Our Hearts

Refrain

Change our hearts this time,
your word says it can be.
Change our minds this time,
your life could make us free.
We are the people, your call set apart,
Lord, this time change our hearts.

1. Brought by your hand
   to the edge of our dreams,
   one foot in paradise, one in the waste;
   drawn by your promises,
   still we are lured by the shadows
   and the chains we leave behind. But . . .

2. Now as we watch you
   stretch out your hands,
   off'ring abundances, fullness of joy.
   Your milk and honey
   seem distant, unreal,
   when we have bread and water
   in our hands. But . . .

3. Show us the way
   that leads to your side,
   over the mountains
   and sands of the soul.
   Be for us manna, water from stone,
   light which says we never walk alone. And . . .

Children of God

1. Children of God,
   That's what we are,
   Called to love ev'ryone
   With our Father's heart.

Refrain

Sisters and brothers of Jesus,
It's plain to see:
There's a strong family resemblance
In God's family.

2. Children of God,
   Strong, loving, wise,
   Called to see ev'rything
   Through our Father's eyes.

3. Children of God,
   Learning God's plans,
   Called to build a better world
   With our Father's hands.

Words and Music by Rory Cooney
Copyright © 2005 by GIA Publications, Inc., 7404 South Mason Ave., Chicago, IL 60638, 800.442.1358 www.giamusic.com. All rights reserved. Printed in the U.S.A.,

Psalm 103 – The Lord Is Kind and Merciful

Refrain

The Lord is kind and merciful.
The Lord is kind and merciful.
The Lord is kind and merciful,
slow to anger, rich in compassion.
The Lord is kind and merciful.

1. My soul, give thanks to the Lord.
   All my being, bless his holy name.
   My soul, give thanks to the Lord
   and never forget all his blessings.

2. It is he who forgives all your guilt,
   who heals every one of your ills,
   who redeems your life from the grave,
   who crowns you with love and compassion.

Text (refrain) © 1969, 1981, ICEL. Text (verses) © 1963, Ladies of the Grail (England). GIA, exclusive agent. Ed Bolduc, Music © 1998, World Library Publications. www.wlpmusic.com. All rights reserved. Used with permission.

Malo! Malo! Thanks Be to God

Refrain

(Cantor intones each phrase. All repeat.)

Malo! Malo!	*[Tongan, mah-loh mah-loh]*
Thanks be to God!	
Obrigado! Alleluia!	*[Portuguese, o-bree-ga-doh]*
¡Gracias!	*[Spanish, grah-see-ahs]*
Kam sa ham ni da!	*[Korean, kahm sah hahm nee dah]*

Malo! Malo! Thanks be to God!
Verses: Cantor; All Repeat

1. Si Yu'us maa'se! *[Chamoru, see joos mah-ah-sih]*

   Terima kasih! *[Indonesian, three-mah kah-seeh]*

   Maraming salamat! *[Tagalog, mah-rah-meeng sah-lah-maht]*

   Danke schön! *[German, dahn-kuh shuhn]*

   Dzi̞ekuj̞e! *[Polish, jehn-koo-yeh]*
   We thank you, Lord!

2. Mèsi bokou! *[Creole, meh-see boh-koo]*
   Xie xie! *[Mandarin, shee-eh shee-eh]*

   Arigatō! *[Japanese, ah-ree-gah-toh]*
   Grazie! *[Italian, grah-tsee-eh]*
   Cám ỏn! *[Vietnamese, gahm urn]*
   We thank you, Lord!

Malo! Malo! Thanks Be To God © 1993, Jesse Manibusan.
Published by spiritandsong.com®, 5536 NE Hassalo, Portland OR 97213.
All rights reserved. Used with permission.

Give Us Your Peace

Refrain

Jesus, give us your peace.
Bring us together.
Let all the fighting cease.
Shatter all our hearts of stone.
Give us a heart for love alone.

1. Some days the road I walk is lonely,
   and it's so hard to find a friend.
   Even then I know, somewhere in my soul,
   your love is far too great to comprehend.

3. Some days the strength I need is failing,
   And then, O Lord, I turn to you.
   I need never fear, you are always near.
   Whatever happens,
       you will pull me through.

I Say "Yes," Lord / Digo "Sí," Señor

1. To the God who cannot die:
   I say "Yes," my Lord.
   To the One who hears me cry:
   Digo "Sí," Señor.
   To the God of the oppressed:
   I say "Yes," my Lord.
   To the God of all justice:
   Digo "Sí," Señor.

Refrain

I say "Yes," my Lord, in all the good times,
   through all the bad times,
I say "Yes," my Lord,
   to ev'ry word you speak.
*Digo "Sí," Señor, en tiempos malos,
   en tiempos buenos,
Digo "Sí," Señor, a todo lo que hablas.*

3. For the dream I have today:
   I say "Yes," my Lord.
   To be a healer of all pain:
   Digo "Sí," Señor.
   To come to love my enemies:
   I say "Yes," my Lord.
   For your peace in all the world:
   Digo "Sí," Señor.

4. Like that of Job, unceasingly:
   I say "Yes," my Lord.
   Like that of Maria wholeheartedly:
   Digo "Sí," Señor.
   Like that of David in a song:
   I say "Yes," my Lord.
   Like Israel, for you I long:
   Digo "Sí," Señor.

Yes, We Believe

1. Do you believe in God, the Father,
   the Almighty,
   maker of heaven and Earth?

Refrain

Yes, we believe, we do, Lord!
Yes, we believe, we do, Lord!
Yes, we believe, we do, Lord!

2. Do you believe in Jesus, God's only Son,
   our Lord,
   who was born of the Virgin Mary,
   was crucified under Pontius Pilate,
   suffered and died, and was buried?

3. Do you believe that on the third day
   he rose from the dead,
   and is now seated at the Father's right hand?

4. Do you believe in the Holy Spirit?
   (Yes, we believe, we do, Lord!)
   In the Lord, the giver of all life?
   (Yes, we believe. . .)
   With the Father and Son, he is worshiped
   and glorified.
   (Yes, we believe. . .)
   He has spoken to us through the Prophets.
   (Yes, we believe. . .)
   Do you believe in the holy catholic Church,
   (Yes, we believe. . .)
   One baptism for the forgiveness of all sin?
   (Yes, we believe. . .)
   Do you believe that the dead shall rise,
   and in life of the world to come? Amen!

Music by Paul A. Tate. Music © 1996, World Library Publications.
www.wlpmusic.com. All rights reserved. Used with permission.

We Are the Body of Christ / Somos El Cuerpo De Cristo

Refrain

Somos el cuerpo de Cristo.
We are the body of Christ.
Hemos oído el llamado;
We've answered "Yes," to the call
of the Lord.
Somos el cuerpo de Cristo.
We are the body of Christ.
Traemos su santo mensaje.
We come to bring the good news
to the world.

1. Cantor: *Dios viene al mundo a través de nosotros.*
   All: **Somos el cuerpo de Cristo.**
   Cantor: God is revealed when we love one another.
   All: **We are the body of Christ.**
   Cantor: *Al mundo a cumplir la misión de la Iglesia,*
   All: **Somos el cuerpo de Cristo.**
   Cantor: Bringing the light of God's mercy to others,
   All: **We are the body of Christ.**

2. Cantor: *Cada persona es parte del reino;*
   All: **Somos el cuerpo de Cristo.**
   Cantor: Putting a stop to all discrimination,
   All: **We are the body of Christ.**
   Cantor: *Todas las razas que habitan la tierra,*
   All: **Somos el cuerpo de Cristo.**
   Cantor: All are invited to feast in the banquet.
   All: **We are the body of Christ.**

Somos El Cuerpo de Cristo © 1994, Jaime Cortez.
Published by OCP Publications, 5536 NE Hassalo, Portland OR 97213.
All rights reserved. Used with permission.

Anthem

Refrain

We are called, we are chosen.
We are Christ for one another.
We are promised to tomorrow,
while we are for him today.
We are sign, we are wonder.
We are sower, we are seed.
We are harvest, we are hunger.
We are question, we are creed.

1. Then where can we stand justified?
   In what can we believe?
   In no one else but Christ who suffered,
   nothing more than Christ who rose.
   Who was justice for the poor.
   Who was rage against the night.
   Who was hope for peaceful people.
   Who was light.

2. Then how are we to stand at all,
   this world of bended knee?
   In nothing more than barren shadows.
   No one else but Christ could save us.
   Who was justice for the poor.
   Who was rage against the night.
   Who was hope for peaceful people.
   Who was light.

Song of the Body of Christ

Refrain

We come to share our story,
we come to break the bread,
we come to know our rising
from the dead.

1. We come as your people,
   we come as your own,
   united with each other,
   love finds a home.

2. We are called to heal the broken,
   to be hope for the poor,
   we are called to feed the hungry
   at our door.

3. Bread of life and cup of promise,
   in this meal we all are one.
   In our dying and our rising,
   may your kingdom come.